2006

For Jacque ~

To add to your exploration into foods of cultures.

Hope you enjoy some of these recipes.

Merry Christmas.

Love,
Mom & Dad

Flavors
of the Philippines

For Pancho, Bito, Bea
and the entire staff of Via Mare
for their invaluable support

FLAVORS OF THE PHILIPPINES

Published in The Philippines by
VIA MARE CATERING SERVICES INC.,
Secretariat Building, Philippine International Convention Center,
CCP Complex, Roxas Boulevard, Manila

Copyright © 1997 Glenda Rosales-Barretto

Project Co-ordinator : John Mitchell
Editorial Consultant : Michaela Fenix
Food photography : Neal Oshima
Destination photography : George Tapan
Food stylist : Jean-Pierre Migné
Art and Studio Designs : Red Creatives Inc., Manila
Business Consultant : Greg Trinidad

ISBN: 971-91882-0-0

Printed in Hong Kong

Flavors
of the Philippines

A Culinary Guide to the Best of the Islands

Glenda Rosales-Barretto

Contents

Foreword

FLAVORS OF THE PHILIPPINES, a Culinary Guide to the Best of the Islands is an expression of my personal commitment to give wider recognition and appreciation to a body of cooking styles and techiques collectively known as Philippine cuisine. Underrated and unknown in some parts of the world, Philippine cookery stands out as one of the most satisfying and comforting foods in this part of the world.

Aboriginal in roots, the trunk is a sturdy mixture of Malay, Chinese and Spanish cookery. The foliage and fruits however of this astonishingly pleasant cuisine is characteristically native in flavor and taste.

Filipino food is a friendly encounter with both the exotic and the familiar. The flavors are sweet and spicy, the tastes fresh and simple, the textures varied and playful, and the colors bright and appetizingly vibrant. Let us take, for example, the Lumpia Ubod. It is a sauté of crisp hearts of palm, with that ever so subtle flavor of coconuts, and fresh succulent shrimps with savory tidbits of pork. The mixture is wrapped with a garden-fresh lettuce leaf and soft velvety egg crepe, and served with a salty, sweet brown sauce, chopped toasted peanuts and finely minced garlic. The presentation is an intricate interplay of flavors and tastes, of colors and textures that pleases almost all the senses.

The recipes in this book have delighted and pleased many, from gourmets to plain folks who love good food. To bring out the best qualities of these recipes be sure to use only the freshest produce and ingredients available, especially the seafood and the vegetables. Use only sea salt and freshly ground peppercorns.

Although this book is but one bouquet from the wide garden of Philippine gastronomy, it is my way of sharing with friends the joys and rewards of cooking Filipino style. And, if somehow it leads you, the reader, to a discovery and appreciation of Philippine cuisine, then the time and effort of putting it together will have been worthwhile.

Weights & Measures

Recipes in this edition have been written using metric measurements. Solids and liquid measurements less than 50 grams (50g) and 50 milliliters (50ml) are generally given in 5g/ml teaspoons (tsp) and 15g/ml tablespoons (tbsp), while larger quantities are generally shown in steps of 25g/ml. Exceptions to the above occur when precise quantities are of the utmost importance. Some vegetables, when whole, are shown in units and, where no reference is made to size, it should be assumed that medium size is called for.

For those preferring to work in cups or Imperial measures, to achieve the best results, it is essential, when converting, to use ingredients in the same proportion those given. 28g/ml is the nearest whole figure equivalent to 1 ounce/fluid ounce.

Many of the following recipes call for the use of coconut cream or coconut milk and it is important, wherever possible, to use fresh coconuts.

To make, grate 2 coconuts and wrap the resulting pulp in cheesecloth. Squeeze to extract 375 ml cream and set this aside. Add 750 ml hot water to the remaining pulp and squeeze again to extract the milk.

Where fresh coconuts are not readily available, use solid packs of creamed coconut (available in most supermarkets) and follow the instructions on the pack to produce either cream or milk. Coconut cream can also be bought in cans or frozen.

Manila Flavors

Metropolitan Manila today is a sprawling urban area of several cities and municipalities. Its beginning, however, was a small enclosed settlement by the Pasig River, a walled fortress called Intramuros. Intramurous today still lives within those same protective walls.

Being at the center of the country, Manila's cosmopolitan atmosphere is reflected in the flavors of its food. *Gambas* is a flavorful dish of shrimps cooked with a chill-garlic sauce and chickens are stuffed as in *rellenong manok*. If in most parts of the country the roast suckling pig, *lechon*, is served as is, in Manila it is stuffed with savory *Paella*.If all these seem lavish, there are also the simple joys such as *sotanghon con caldo*, a Chinese-influenced dish of noodles and broth.

While the refreshing *halo-halo,* filled with sweets and crushed ice and enriched with milk, is found everywhere, it is never more appreciated than in Manila, especially in the hot summer months.

SOTANGHON con CALDO (mung bean noodle soup)

*150 g sotanghan
  (mung bean noodles)*
2 tbsp oil
2 tbsp chopped garlic
4 tbsp chopped onion
200 g chicken breast, sliced
2.5 liters stock (see below)
*6 wood ear mushrooms
  soaked and cut into strips*
50 g julienne carrot
patis (fish sauce) to taste
freshly ground white pepper

100 g cabbage, julienned
1 tbsp chopped spring onion

Stock:
500 g ham bones
1 kilo chicken parts
2 leeks, sliced
1 large onion, chopped
3 stalks celery, sliced
1 tsp black peppercorns

Soak the noodles in water for at least 10 minutes, then cut into 5 cm lengths.

Heat the oil in a casserole and fry the garlic, then remove and reserve. Add onion, chicken and stock and bring to the boil. Allow to simmer for 5 minutes, then season with fish sauce and pepper.

Add the noodles, together with the woodear and carrot and continue to simmer for 10 minutes, then add the cabbage and cook for a further minute. Transfer to a soup tureen and top with spring onion and crispy-fried garlic.

To make the stock, place all the ingredients in a large pot and add 3 litres of water. Bring to the boil, then cover the pot, lower heat and allow to simmer for 90 minutes. Pass through a fine strainer and set aside. Discard solids.

GAMBAS (shrimps in chili garlic sauce)

300 g fresh shrimps
1 tbsp fresh calamansi juice
sea salt to taste
freshly ground black pepper
1 tsp sweet paprika

75 ml olive oil
3 tbsp minced garlic
*2 chili peppers,
  finely chopped*
liquid savory seasoning to taste

Wash shrimps in calamansi juice, then drain and season with salt, pepper and paprika.

Heat the oil in a pan and sauté the garlic until golden brown, then add shrimps, chili pepper and liquid seasoning. Cook over high heat, very briefly, to prevent the release of the shrimp juices. Serve immediately.

LAPU LAPU EN MAYONESA (steamed garoupa with mayonnaise)

1.5 kilos red lapu-lapu (grouper)
1 tbsp sea salt
1 tsp freshly ground pepper
1 tbsp fresh calamansi juice
30 g leeks, julienned
20 g ginger, julienned
150 g mayonnaise

Garnish:
2 hard boiled eggs, whites and
  yolks chopped separately
100 g boiled carrots, finely chopped
100 g pickle relish, chopped
3 tbsp chopped parsley

Clean and scale the fish and season with salt, pepper and calamsi juice.

Top the fish with leek and ginger and cook in a steamer for 20-25 minutes. Set aside to cool, then chill in the refrigerator.

When ready to serve, remove the skin from the fish, arrange on a platter, coat evenly with mayonnaise and garnish with alternating layers of egg, carrot, relish and parsley.

RELLENONG MANOK (stuffed chicken)

1 chicken, approx. 1.2 kilos
1 tsp sea salt
0.5 tsp freshly ground pepper
125 g Vienna sausage, chopped
100 g Chorizo Bilbao
 (garlic sausage), chopped
150 g onions,chopped

100 g canned pimiento, finely diced
50 g stuffed olives, sliced
3 tbsp raisins
3 tbsp grated edam cheese
1 egg, lightly beaten
5 hard boiled eggs
butter for brushing

Prepare the chicken and carefully de-bone (see below), then season inside and out with salt and pepper.

In a mixing bowl, combine the remaining ingredients, apart from the hard boiled eggs and butter. Season to taste and mix well.

Stuff the mixture inside the chicken and arrange the hard boiled eggs in the center by pushing the mixture along the sides of the cavity.

Sew the opening securely with kitchen thread, using overlapping stitches. (Do not sew too tightly or the chicken with burst during cooking.)

Soften the butter and brush over the chicken, then bake in a pre-heated, moderate oven for at least 1 hour, until the chicken is cooked and the skin is-golden brown.

To de-bone, place the chicken on its back and, from the open cavity, ease a small, sharp paring knife between the flesh and bone structure. Start detaching the breast meat from the backbone and continue to work to the leg joints, turning the bird around as you proceed. Separate the legs from the bone structure and cut off at the joints. Detach leg bones from the flesh up to the base and cut off bones. Separate wings from the bone structure, cutting at the joints but leaving bones intact. Continue to cut flesh from bone up to the neck. Finally, clasp the neckbone at the base, pull out the bone structure until the whole carcass is free.

LECHON DE LECHE RELLENADO (stuffed roast suckling pig)

5 kilo whole suckling pig,
* cleaned and prepared*
1 tbsp sea salt
1 tbsp freshly ground pepper
1 tbsp minced garlic
paella (see following recipe)
oil for basting

Liver sauce:
250 g pork liver
75 ml vinegar

2 tbsp oil
2 tsp minced garlic
2 tbsp chopped onion
1 liter chicken stock
2 tsp soy sauce
2 tbsp sea salt
1 tbsp freshly ground pepper
1 bay leaf
100 g breadcrumbs

Rub the entire cavity of the pig with salt, pepper and garlic, then spoon in the rice. Sew opening with kitchen thread using overlapping stitches. Brush the skin with oil and roast in a preheated oven, 180° C, for 90 minutes, basting with oil every 15 minutes, then increase heat to 200° C and continue to roast for a further 30 minutes. Serve with a liver sauce.

To make the sauce, briefly broil the liver, then pass the liver through a food processor while pouring in the vinegar in a slow, steady stream.

Heat the oil in a pan and sauté the garlic and onion for 2-3 minutes, then add the processed liver, stock, soy sauce, salt, pepper and bay leaf.

Bring to the boil, then reduce heat and allow to simmer for 10 minutes. Finally, add the breadcrumbs, adjust seasonings and stir until the sauce thickens.

PAELLA MANILENA

PAELLA MANILENA (savory rice with seafoods)

100 g slab of bacon, cubed
2 tbsp olive oil
50 g minced garlic
100 g diced onion
200 g tomatoes, peeled, seeded
  and chopped
100 g red and green bell pepper,
  cut into strips
75 g chorizo Bilbao (garlic sausage)
  sliced diagonally
2 tbsp paprika
2 bay leaves
100 g white fish sticks
100 g squid, skinned and scored
2 crabs, quartered
100 g clams

150 g mussels
6 medium size prawns,
  heads removed
450 g long grain rice
1.25 liters chicken stock
50 g green beans
sea salt to taste
freshly ground peppercorns

Garnish
2 hard boiled eggs,
  cut into wedges
50 g cooked peas
2 Tbsp black olives
2 tsp chopped parsley
1 lemon, cut into wedges

In a heavy pan, preferably a paellera, heat the olive oil and fry the bacon until the fat is rendered, then remove bacon and drain on kitchen paper.

Add to the pan, the garlic, onion, tomato, bell peppers, bacon and sausage and sauté for 3-4 minutes, then add paprika, bay leaves and seafoods. Simmer for 2 minutes, then remove seafoods and set aside.

Add rice and stock to the pan and season to taste with salt and pepper. Cook until the rice is almost done, then replace the seafoods and add the green beans. Cover pan with a tightly fitting lid and cook until the liquid has been absorbed by the rice, approximately 20 minutes

Transfer to a large serving platter and garnish with eggs, peas, olive, parsley and lemon wedges.

NOTE: When the paella is to be used as stuffing for **roast suckling pig,** omit
      crabs and remove shells from clams, mussels and prawns.

HALO HALO (melange of sweetened fruit and pulses)

*250 g red monggo (mung) beans,
   soaked overnight*
*250 white beans,
   soaked overnight*
*250 g macapuno (coconut),
   cut into strips*
*6 saba (cooking bananas),
   sliced horizontally*
*250 g nangka (jackfruit),
   cut into strips*

1.8 kilos sugar
1 bar red gulaman (jelly)
*100 g haleyang ube (see page 41)
   cut into small cubes*
*100 g coco flan (see page 51)
   cut into small pieces*
250 ml evaporated milk
*ube (purple yam) or macapuno
   ice-cream, optional*

Place the red beans in a saucepan, add 750 ml water and boil for 30 minutes, or until tender, then add 500 g sugar and simmer for a further 30 minutes. Place the white beans in another saucepan, add 1 liter water and boil for 1 hour, or until tender, then add 500 g sugar and simmer for a further 30 minutes.

To cook the fruits, use 3 separate pans and place 250 g sugar in each. For the coconut add 175 ml water, for the bananas add 250 ml water and for the jackfruit add just 75 ml water. Bring each to the boil and simmer for 3 minutes, then add respective fruits and cook over a low heat for 10 minutes.

Place the jelly bar in a pan and cover with 450 ml water. Soak for 10 minutes, then add 50 g sugar and boil until jelly has completely dissolved. Chill to set and cut into small cubes.

To serve, arrange layers of prepared ingredients in tall glasses and top with shaved ice. Pour in a little evaporated milk. If desired, add a scoop of ice-cream.

TURONES DE SABA (fried banana rolls)

12 ripe saba (coooking bananas)
150 ripe nangka (jackfruit)
200 g brown sugar

48 lumpia (spring roll) wrappers)
oil for deep frying

Peel the bananas and slice, lengthwise, into 4 pieces. Roll the slices in sugar. Cut the jackfruit into 48 strips.

Place a banana slice and a strip of jackfruit in the center of a wrapper, then roll up and secure

Heat the oil until medium hot, then deep-fry the rolls until golden and crispy.

19

Central Luzon Flavors

From its vast plains, swamp lands and rivers, Central Luzon has a plethora of nature's bounties. And, as though nature knew that only gourmet cooking can do justice to them, migratory ducks, wild boars and snipes abound.

Here, it is Pampango cuisine that is best known for its flavorful and lavish cooking. The flavor of its dishes are always rich, vigorous and distinctive.

Fiestas in Pampanga are eagerly anticipated gastronomic events, and food lovers come from far afield to enjoy the fare. The master cooks, respected for their culinary skills, outdo each other with their own savory versions of such dishes as *caldereta, morcon, relleno, adobo* and many, many more. Fiesta is also the time for such sweet delights as *tibok-tibok, pichi-pichi, yema* and *leche flan*.

ADOBONG SUGPO sa TABA ng TALANGKA
(stewed prawns in crabfat sauce)

1 kilo fresh prawns,
1 tbsp minced garlic
1 tsp fresly ground pepper
125 ml vinegar
75 ml soy sauce

2 bay leaves
75 g taba ng talangka
  (crabfat paste)
250 ml oil for frying
1 tbsp crispy-fried garlic slivers

Shell and de-vein the prawns, leaving head and tails intact

Place prawns, garlic, pepper, vinegar, soy sauce and bay leaves in a pan and add 250 ml water, Bring to the boil, then reduce heat and leave to simmer for 10 minutes.

Remove prawns and set aside. Strain the sauce and return to the pan, then stir in the crabfat paste. Set aside. Heat the oil and fry the prawns for 45 seconds, then remove, drain on absorbent paper and arrange on a serving platter.

Reheat the sauce, pour over the prawns and garnish with fried garlic.

INIHAW ɴᴀ DALAG ᴀᴛ BURO (mudfish with fermented rice)

600 g dalag (mudfish)
1 tsp seasalt
0.25 tsp freshly ground pepper
2 tbsp olive oil
150 g onions, finely chopped
1 tbsp minced garlic

200 g tomatoes, chopped
250 g burong isda
*   (fermented rice)*
300 g eggplant, broiled
300 g ampalaya (bittermelon),
*   sliced diagonally and broiled*
200 g fresh mustard leaves

Butterfly the mudfish, remove center bones, and season with salt and pepper. Broil the fish, flesh side first, for approximately 5 minutes on each side, then transfer to a large serving platter.

Meanwhile, heat the oil in a pan and sauté the garlic, onion and tomato for 5 minutes, then add the fermented rice and 150 ml water. Mix well and bring to the boil, then lower heat. Allow to simmer for 20 minutes, then transfer to a sauce bowl

Surround the fish with the broiled vegetables and mustard leaves and serve with the sauce.

KARE-KARENG BUNTOT (ox tail in peanut annato sauce)

1 piece ox tail, use middle portion, approximately 30 cm length
2.5 tbsp minced garlic
175 g onions, quartered
1 tsp freshly ground pepper
2 bay leaves
400 g banana hearts, quartered
100 g string beans, cut into 5 cm lengths

2 large eggplants, cut diagonally
250 g pechay (Chinese cabbage)
2 tbsp annato oil
1 small onion, chopped
3 large tomatoes, peeled, seeded and chopped
125 g rice flour, toasted
125 g peanuts, toasted and ground

Place the oxtail, 1.5 tbsp garlic, the onion, peppercorns and bay leaves in a large pot and add sufficient water to cover, then bring to the boil and cook until the meat is tender, approximately 4-5 hours. Strain the liquid into a fresh container and set aside. Keep meat warm in the pot.

Heat the annato oil in a casserole and sauté the onion, tomato and remaining garlic for 3-4 minutes, then add the reserved liquid and bring to the boil. Add the banana heart and cook for 5 minutes, then add the beans, eggplant and cabbage. Cook for a further 5 minutes, then remove vegetables from the casserole and set aside.

While still warm, de-bone the oxtail, cutting lengthwise, and stuff with some vegetables. Roll tightly into a cylinder and wrap in plastic film, then cover with aluminum foil and chill in the refrigerator.

Add the rice flour and ground peanuts to the liquid in the casserole and bring to boiling point, stirring continuously until the sauce reaches a thick, but flowing consistency. Keep hot.

Unwrap and slice the oxtail. Reheat in a steamer and arrange on a large serving platter. Surround with vegetables and top with the thick sauce. Serve with a side dish of sautéed shrimp paste.

ESTOPADONG DILA (braised ox tongue)

1.5 kilos ox tongue
3 tbsp soy sauce
125 ml cooking oil
1 small onion, chopped
200 g tomatoes, peeled and chopped
2 tbsp minced garlic
1 chorizo Bilbao (garlic sausage)
2 bay leaves

75 ml red wine
1.25 liters beef stock
125 g button mushrooms
12 stuffed green olives
sea salt to taste
freshly ground pepper
5 saba (cooking bananas),
*   cut in half diagonally and fried*

Scald the tongue in boiling water until the skin turns white, then rinse in cold water and scrape outer membranes with the edge of a knife. Rub with 1 tbsp soy sauce.

Heat the oil in a large casserole and brown the ox tongue, then pour off excess oil, add onion, tomato, garlic, sausage, bay leaves, wine, stock and remaining soy sauce and bring to the boil..

Lower heat, cover and allow to simmer for 1 hour. Remove the sausage, slice diagonally and set aside. Continue to cook until tongue is tender, then remove and slice into serving-size pieces.

Strain the liquid and return to the casserole, together with the tongue, sausage, mushrooms and olives. Simmer for a further 10-15 minutes, then transfer to a serving plate and garnish with fried banana.

KARE - KARENG BUNTOT

SISIG (minced pork relish)

500 g hog's head,
  cleaned and de-boned
2 tbsp minced garlic
75 ml soy sauce
125 ml vinegar
1 bay leaf
1 tbsp sea salt
1 tsp freshly ground pepper
oil for frying
2 tbsp finely chopped spring onion

Sauce:
150 g cooked chicken livers,
125 ml vinegar
60 ml fresh calamansi juice
2 tbsp chopped chili pepper
1 tsp freshly ground black pepper
1 tsp sea salt

Place the meat, garlic, soy sauce, vinegar, bay leaf, salt and pepper in a medium casserole and add 1.25 liters of water. Bring to the boil, then lower heat and leave to simmer for 2 hours, or until the meat is tender.

Remove the meat and cut into 5 mm slices, then broil for 1 minute on each side. Then, deep fry in very hot oil until crispy.

Drain the meat on absorbent paper and chop coarsley, then add the sauce and mix well. Transfer to a dish and sprinkle with finely chopped spring onion.

To make the sauce, mash the chicken liver with vinegar and calamansi juice to a coarse paste. Add the chili, salt and pepper and blend thoroughly.

ENSALADANG PAKO (fiddlehead fern salad)

100 g fresh shrimps
300 g pako (fiddlehead fern),
  tender parts only, 5 cm lengths
2 salted duck eggs
  shelled and cut into wedges
1 small onion, sliced
1 large tomato, cut into wedges

Vinaigrette:
2 tbsp fresh calamansi juice
1 tbsp bagoong isda
  (anchovy sauce)
75 ml olive oil
0.5 tsp freshly ground pepper

Steam the shrimps, then shell and de-vein.

Blanch the fern and immediately immerse in cold water. Drain and shake off excess liquid. Place fern in a salad bowl, add shrimps, eggs, onion, and tomato and toss lightly, then drizzle generously with the vinaigrette.

To make the vinaigrette, mix together all the ingredients and shake well.

PICHI-PICHI (sticky rice balls)

375 ml coconut cream
500 g pinipig (pounded sticky rice)
100 g granulated sugar

1 pandan leaf
50 g softened butter
100 g grated coconut

Pour the coconut cream into a deep saucepan and bring to the boil. Add rice, sugar and pandan leaf and reduce heat.

Stir continuously over a low heat until the mixture holds together and starts to separate from the pan, then mix in the butter and remove pan from the heat. Discard the pandan leaf

Allow to cool, then form into bite-size balls and roll in grated coconut.

TIBOK-TIBOK (cream of water buffalo milk)

125 g rice flour
75 g granulated sugar
750 ml coconut cream
500 ml buffalo milk

50 ml condensed milk
75 g softened butter
oil from 1 medium size dayap rind
  (native lime)

Place rice in a heavy pan, add 125 ml water and simmer until mixture thickens, then add sugar and coconut cream.

Stir over a low heat for 10 minutes, then add the buffalo milk, condensed milk, butter and dayap oil and continue stirring until mixture coats spoon.

Pour into a shallow pan and allow to set in the refrigerator.

YEMA (custard bonbons)

750 ml condensed milk
12 egg yolks

500 g granulated sugar

Place milk and egg yolks in a double boiler and cook, stirring continuously, until mixture holds together and starts to separate from the pan. Cool, then shape into bite-size balls and set aside.

In a saucepan, heat sugar over a moderate heat until it melts and starts to turn golden brown, then remove pan from heat.

Using toothpicks, dip the yema balls into the hot syrup and transfer to a greased pan. Occasionally reheat syrup to ensure it remains at melting point.

Northern Luzon Flavors

The Ifugao rice terraces, considered the eighth wonder of the world, are carved out of the mountains, a testament to the ingenuity of our ancient tribes. The mountain people of the rice terraces and the Ilocanos of the northern region are hardy folk and they live on what their arid lands offer. Their cuisine, as a result, is basic, but nourishing.

Ilocano cooking is popular all over the Philippines and its very simplicity is its own virtue. For example, *baradibud*, a fresh vegetable stew in sweet potato broth, is a gustatory pleasure too good to be missed. And, *pinakbet*, a vegetable stew with crisp pork belly, is a staple item in most local restaurants.

The bitter dishes are a facet of gastronomy unexplored by many. Purposely laced into meat stews, fish broils and salads, the bitter taste is savored as a quality as enjoyable as the other aspects of taste, such as sweet, sour and salty.

RELLENONG BANGUS (stuffed milkfish)

500 g whole milkfish
1 tbsp fresh calamansi juice
1 tbsp soy sauce
freshly ground black pepper
1 bay leaf
1.5 tbsp finely chopped celery
75 g chopped onion
2 tbsp oil
4 cloves garlic, minced
1 tomato, skined, seeded
  and chopped
75 g green peas
75 g raisins

1 egg, lightly beaten
75 g grated parmesan cheese
sea salt to taste
banana leaves (optional)

Sauce:

1 tbsp olive oil
1tsp minced garlic
2 tbsp chopped onion
2 tomatoes, skinned and chopped
2 tbsp cooked green peas
sea salt to taste
freshly ground pepper

With the side of a kitchen knife, gently pound the fish to loosen the meat from the skin, then break the big bone at the neck. Through the neck, insert the handle of a tablespoon and carefully scrape the meat from the skin, pushing towards the tail. Break bone at the tail end and pull out and reserve the meat.

Lay the skin in a shallow dish, add calamansi juice, soy sauce and pepper and set aside for 20 minutes.

Place the bayleaf, celery and half the onion in a saucepan, add 500 ml water and bring to the boil. Reduce heat and simmer for 5 minutes, then add the fish meat and simmer for a further 5 minutes. Strain and reserve the stock. Carefully remove the bones, then flake the meat.

Heat the oil in a fresh saucepan and sauté the garlic, then add remaining onion and tomato, cook for 3 minutes, then add the peas, raisins and fish meat. Season to taste and cook for a further 5-6 minutes.

Allow the mixture to cool, then add stir in the egg and cheese. Stuff the mixture inside the marinated skin and brush the outside with oil.

Place in a baking pan greased with butter or lined with banana leaves and bake in a pre-heated, moderate oven until the skin is golden brown.

Transfer to a platter and serve with the sauce.

To make the sauce, heat the oil in a pan and sauté the garlic, onion and tomato for 3 minutes, then add 250 ml reserved broth. Simmer for 10 minutes, then add the peas and season to taste.

RELLENONG BANGUS - ENSALADANG BAGNET

KALDERETA (spicy mutton stew)

1 kilo fresh mutton	2 bay leaves
75 ml red wine	1 tsp paprika
125 ml cooking oil	250 g tomato sauce
1.5 tbsp minced garlic	12 liter beef stock
100 g onion, diced	sea salt to taste
200 g tomatoes, sliced	freshly ground black pepper
100 g diced red bell pepper	75 g liver spread
100 g diced green bell pepper	50 g green stuffed olives
2 tsp finely chopped chili pepper	1 tbsp grated Edam cheese
2 tbsp soy sauce	50 g pimientos, cut into strips

Cut meat into serving-size pieces and marinate in red wine for at least 2 hours, then drain meat and set aside. Reserve the marinade.

In a saucepan, heat the oil and brown the meat on all sides in batches. Transfer meats as they brown to a platter. Pour excess oil from pan, leaving only about 3 tbsp. Fry garlic, then add onion, tomato, bell peppers and chilli peppers and sauté for 3 minutes.

Add the reserved marinade, bay leaves, paprika, tomato sauce, soy sauce, beef stock and replace the meat. Bring to the boil, then lower heat and simmer for 1 hour. Stir in the liver spread, add olives, cheese, salt and pepper and cook for a further 2 minutes. Transfer to a serving dish and garnish with pimiento strips.

IGADO (ragout of pork liver)

1 kilo pork liver, heart and kidney,
  thinly sliced
75 ml annato oil
2 tsp minced garlic
100 g chopped onion
3 bay leaves
1 tsp freshly ground black pepper

75 ml soy sauce
250 ml vinegar
500 ml meat stock
1 red bell pepper, cut into strips
1 green bell pepper, cut into strips
125 g cooked green peas
1 tbsp sea salt

Heat the oil in a pan and sauté the garlic until brown, then add meats, onion, bay leaves, pepper and soy sauce.

Continue to sauté until the liquid has completely reduced, then add vinegar and allow to simmer for 15 minutes.

Add stock, bell peppers, peas and salt and continue to simmer until the meats are tender. Serve immediately.

ENSALADANG BAGNET
(pork crackling with tomato and seaweed salad)

300 g bagnet (pork belly crackling)
  (see following page)
150 g shallots, slivered
500 g tomatoes, cut into wedges
1 tbsp chopped kinchay
  (Chinese parsley)

2 tbsp fresh calamansi juice
3 tbsp bagoong isda
  (anchovy sauce), strained
2 tsp freshly ground black pepper
250 g seaweed

Chop the crackling into bite-size chunks.

In a bowl, mix the shallot, tomato, parsley, anchovy sauce calamansi juice and pepper, then add the crackling and toss lightly.

Transfer to a salad bowl and arrange the seaweed around the sides.

PINAKBET (vegetable stew)

300 g bagnet, sliced (see below)
2 tsp oil
2 tsp chopped ginger
1.5 tbsp crushed garlic
150 g shallots
500 g ripe tomatoes
75 ml bagoong isda
* (anchovy sauce), strained*
150 g okra

150 g small ampalaya (bittermelon),
* quartered*
300 g eggplants, sliced

Bagnet:
1 kilo pork belly (whole piece)
50 g crushed garlic
2 bay leaves
1 tbsp sea salt

Heat the oil in a casserole and saute the ginger, garlic, shallots, tomatoes and pork crackling until the liquid has completely reduced, then add anchovy sauce. From this point on do not stir.

Continue to simmer until the sauce is thick, then add the okra, bittermelon and eggplant, cover the casserole and cook for a further 5 minutes.

To make the bagnet, place the pork belly, garlic, bay leaves and salt in a pot, add sufficient water to cover and cook for 1 hour. Remove pork and dry in a moderately hot oven for 20 minutes.

Deep fry pork in oil at low heat for at least 1 hour, turning every 15 minutes, then remove and allow to cool completely. To finish, re-heat oil until moderately hot and deep fry the pork until crisp and golden brown.

BARADIBUD (vegetables in sweet potato broth)

600 g camote (sweet potatoes),
* cubed*
100 g onions, diced
300 g tomatoes, diced
400g fresh lima beans
50 g ginger, crushed

100 g chicharon
* (pork skin crackling)*
4 tbsp bagoong isda
* (anchovy sauce)*
100 g string bean tops
100 g squash tops
100 g squash flowers

Place the sweet potato, onion, tomato, beans, ginger, pork and anchovy sauce in a pot and add 1.5 liters water. Bring to the boil, then reduce heat and allow to simmer for 20 minutes.

Add vegetable tops and squash flowers and cook for a further minute, then remove from heat and transfer to a serving dish.

PASTEL DE POLLO (chicken in pastry crust)

1.5 kilo chicken, deboned
* and cut into chunks*
1 tbsp soy sauce
1 tbsp fresh calamansi juice
2 onions, diced
sprig of parsley
125 ml olive oil
100 g slab of bacon,
* cut into 2 cm cubes*
1 tbsp minced garlic
300 g tomatoes,
* skinned and chopped*
100 g Vienna sausage,
* cut into 2 cm slices*

100 g carrots, cubed
100 g potatoes, cubed
100 g champignon mushrooms
50 g stuffed olives
300 g chicken livers, quartered
* and blanched in boiling water*
2 tbsp butter
2 tbsp flour

Crust:
200 g all-purpose flour
100 g butter
1 egg, beaten
eggwash for brushing

Marinate the chicken chunks in soy sauce and calamansi juice for 30 minutes, then drain and discard marinade.

Boil the chicken bones, with salt, pepper, carrot peel, parsley, half the onion and 1 liter water until liquid is reduced by half, then strain stock and set aside.

In a casserole, fry bacon in olive oil to render fat, then remove bacon and set aside. Brown the chicken, a few pieces at a time, in remaining fat, then remove and place with bacon.

Pour away excess oil from the casserole, leaving about 3 tbsp. Sauté garlic and remaining onion, then add tomatoes.Continue to cook until liquids are reduced, then add chicken, bacon, sausage, carrot, potato and half the stock. Bring to the boil, then reduce heat and allow to simmer for 10 minutes. Add mushrooms, olives, chicken livers and cook for a further minute.

Meanwhile, melt the butter in a pan, add the flour and mix well. Add remaining stock and stir until the flour is thoroughly cooked, then stir into the casserole. Remove from heat and transfer to a 2 liter baking dish.

To make the crust, place the flour in a bowl and cut in the butter. Work with the fingers until the mixture resembles bread crumbs, then add the egg and toss lightly with a fork until dough holds together. Roll out dough between plastic sheets to a size approximately 25 mm larger than the baking dish, then remove plastic and place on the dish. Pinch edges of crust, brush top with eggwash, make slits to allow steam to escape and bake in a pre-heated oven at 200° C for 15 minutes, until crust turns golden brown

HALEYANG UBE (purple yam pudding)

1 kilo ube (purple yam)
250 g sugar
750 ml coconut milk

250 ml condensed milk
125 g butter

Boil the yam until tender and cut into cubes, then grind in a food processor with the sugar and coconut milk.

Transfer to a heavy pan, add the condensed milk and butter and cook over a low heat, stirring continuously, until the mixture holds together and starts separating from the pan.

Transfer to a shallow, 20 cm x 50 cm pan lined with plastic film and allow to cool. Slice and serve.

BUKAYO (coconut sweetmeat)

250 ml coconut milk
200 muscovado sugar

pinch of anise
200 g buko (young coconut) meat

In a heavy saucepan, combine the coconut milk, sugar and anise and cook over a low heat, stirring continuously, until the mixture thickens.

Add the coconut meat and cook until mixture is firm, then allow to cool slightly before dividing into individual sweetmeats.

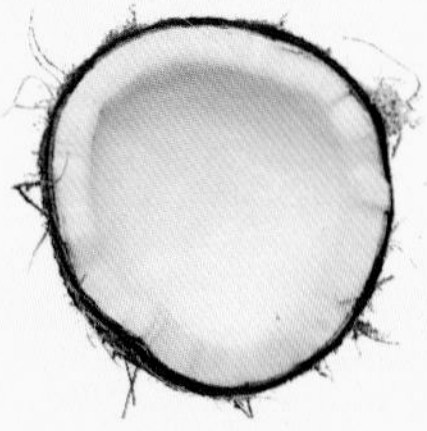

Southern Luzon Flavors

Taal Lake, located in Batangas province, is a volcano that has a volcano within, and the lake itself is the caldera of yet another volcano. Not hard to imagine in a country that lies fully within the Pacific ring of fire.

As in all volcanic places the land is fertile and the waters of the Taal lake yield some of the best tasting freshwater fish.

Batangas is known for its beef industry, so it is no wonder that *bulalo*, beef shank in onion broth and *bistek tagalog*, beef tenderloin in soy and calamansi sauce, are among the best known dishes.

Another province of the southern Tagalog region is Laguna and its economy depends to a great extent on the coconut tree. *Kesong puti*, a popular white cheese made from carabao's milk is produced here.

PINAIS NA ALIMASAG (stuffed crab broiled in banana leaves)

1 kilo crabs
2 tbsp cooking oil
1 tbsp minced garlic
1 tbsp minced ginger
50 g chopped onion
2 tsp finely chopped chili pepper

150 g buko (young coconut) meat,
* cut into fine strips*
175 ml coconut cream
patis (fish sauce) to taste
freshly ground black pepper
banana leaves

Steam the crabs, then allow to cool and flake the meat Reserve the shells.

Heat the oil in a pan and sauté the garlic, ginger and onion for 3 minutes, then add the chili, coconut strips and cream and bring to boiling point. Immediately reduce heat and allow to simmer, stirring continuously until the sauce thickens.

Add the crabmeat and season to taste with fish sauce and pepper, then stuff mixture into the shells. Wrap in banana leaves and tie securely, then broil until the leaves are seared. Transfer to a platter and serve immediately.

ADOBONG PUGO (quail stewed in garlic, vinegar and soy sauce)

12 dressed pugo (quails)
75 ml soy sauce
125 ml vinegar
1 tbsp minced garlic

3 bay leaves
0.5 tsp black peppercorns
50 g pork fat, chopped
oil for frying

Arrange the quails in a casserole, add the soy sauce, vinegar, garlic, bay leaves, peppercorns and pork and leave to marinate for at least 1 hour.

Add water to cover and bring to the boil, then reduce heat and allow to simmer for 1 hour. Remove quails from the sauce and allow to dry.

Heat the oil until moderately hot and deep-fry the quails, then remove, allow to cool and de-bone carefully, keeping the breasts intact. Transfer to a platter.

Re-heat the sauce and simmer until it reaches a desired consistency, then pour over the quails and serve immediately.

BULALO (beef shank in onion broth)

1 kilo beef shank, bone in,
  pre-cut with marrow
500 g beef kneecap
250 g onions, quartered
1 tbsp black peppercorns

sea salt to taste
400 g corn cobs,
  cut into bite-size lengths
300 g pechay (Chinese cabbage),
300 g cabbage, quartered

Place the beef shank, kneecap, onion, peppercorns and salt in a large pot and add sufficient water to cover. Bring to the boil, then reduce heat and allow to simmer for approximately 5 hours, until meat and cartilage begin to separate from the bone.

Add the corn and cook for 20 minutes, then add the cabbage and continue to cook for a further 10 minutes. Transfer to a large dish and serve with a mixture of fish sauce and fresh calamansi juice.

BISTEK TAGALOG (beef tenderloin with calamansi and onion)

500 g beef tenderloin
75 ml olive oil
125 g onions, sliced into rings
125 ml soy sauce
2 tbsp fresh calamansi juice

75 ml beef stock
0.5 tbsp freshly ground pepper
1 tbsp butter
fresh coriander leaves

Cut beef into 15 cm slices and pan-fry in moderately hot oil, a few slices at a time, to desired doneness, then transfer to a serving platter.

Add the onion to the pan and cook until transparent, then add the soy sauce, calamansi juice, stock and pepper. Bring to a low boil and whisk in the butter.

Pour sauce over the meat and garnish with fresh coriander leaves.

ENSALADANG AMPALAYA (bittermelon salad)

400 g ampalaya (bittermelon)
1 tbsp sea salt
150 g cooked shrimps,
  shelled and de-veined
1 large onion, sliced
2 salted duck eggs
  cut into thin wedges

1 tbsp vinegar
3 tbsp olive oil
0.5 tsp granulated sugar
sea salt to taste
freshly ground black pepper
tomato wedges for garnish

Cut the bittermelon in half lengthwise and remove the white pith and seeds, then cut diagonally into thin slices. Mash with salt and squeeze out bitter liquid, then wash well in running water, squeeze dry and place in a salad bowl. Add the shrimps, onion and duck eggs.

Prepare a vinaigrette with the vinegar, olive oil, sugar, salt and pepper and add to the salad bowl. Combine well and garnish with tomato wedges.

ENSALADANG KESONG PUTI AT KAMATIS
(farmers cheese and tomato salad)

Lemon herb dressing:
1 tsp finely chopped fresh basil
125 ml olive oil
1 tbsp balsamic vinegar
1 tbsp fresh lemon juice
sea salt to taste
freshly ground pepper

300 g kesong puti (farmers cheese)
300 g salad tomatoes
200 g lettuce
2 tbsp chopped black olives
1 tbsp finely chopped red and
  green bell peppers

Place the basil, olive oil, vinegar, lemon juice, salt and pepper in a bowl and mix well.

Cut the cheese into slices, 4 cm square and 5 mm thick. Cut the tomatoes into wheels.

Bed a serving platter with lettuce and top with cheese and tomato, then drizzle generously with the prepared dressing. Garnish with olives and bell peppers.

BUKO EN PASTEL (young coconut pie)

Crust:
375 g all-purpose flour
150 g granulated sugar
pinch of sea salt
300 g butter
3 egg yolks

Filling:
3 egg yolks
125 g granulated sugar
2 tbsp cornstarch
250 ml buko (coconut water)
125 ml all purpose cream
450 g buko (coconut meat)
1 tbsp vanilla extract

In a bowl mix the flour, sugar and salt. Cut the butter into into pieces and rub lightly into the flour until the mixture resembles fine breadcrumbs. Add the egg yolks and stir with a round-bladed knife until mixture begins to stick together to form a ball, then knead lightly for a few seconds. Dust the work surface and rolling pin with flour and roll out 75 percent of dough to line a 23 cm baking pan. Place pan in a moderately hot, pre-heated (200° C) oven and bake until lightly browned. Roll out remaining dough for the top and set aside.

To make the filling, whisk the egg yolks and sugar in a large bowl until thick, then add cornstarch and beat in the coconut water. Place the cream and coconut meat in a saucepan and heat until almost boiling, then add the egg mixture and stir well until the mixture boils. Add the vanilla, remove pan from heat and set aside to cool.

Pour the filling into the pastry shell. Cover with the remaining dough and crimp edges to seal. Bake in a moderately hot pre-heated oven (200° C) oven for 25 minutes.

COCO FLAN (coconut cream caramel)

450 g granulated sugar
200 g buko (young cocout) meat
500 ml coconut cream
750 ml evaporated milk

5 eggs
10 egg yolks
2 tbsp vanilla extract
1 tsp lime zest

Caramelize 250 g sugar over a low heat in a heavy saucepan, then pour to coat the bottom of a 2 liter baking pan.

In a blender, purée the coconut meat with the cream and set aside. Combine the evaporated milk, eggs, vanilla, lime zest and remaining sugar in a bowl, then add the puréed coconut. Mix well and strain into the caramel-coated pan.

Bake in a bain-marie in a moderate, pre-heated oven (180° C) for 1 hour, then reduce heat to 140° C and continue to make for a further 15 minutes. Allow to cool before unmolding to a serving platter.

Palawan Flavors

For a long time, Palawan remained unexplored territory. Its bountiful resources in sea and land, its natural beauty, rich vegetation, abundant wildlife were known to only a few. Having been recently "discovered", it has become the destination of choice for those lured by its eco-tourism programs and luxury resorts. New
settlers who long for wild, undeveloped expanses of land, still virgin forests, uninhabited islands and clean air and water have chosen to make these elongated islands their home.

Many of the region's dishes borrow from Visayan cuisine, such as the recipe for *alimango sa labong at saluyot,* crabs with bamboo shoots and wild spinach. The popular chicken stew with sea cucumber, *manok at trepang*, is originally from Mindanao.

A distinct characteristic of Palawan cuisine is the practice of using green mangos to create the sour taste, so enjoyed throughout the Philippines. The recipe for *talakitok at maya-maya sinigang sa mangga*, a combination of red snapper and cavalla in just such a sour broth, is an example.

ALIMANGO sa LABONG at SALUYOT
(crabs with bamboo shoot and wild spinach)

2 kilos crabs, quartered
400 g labong (bamboo shoots)
100 g onion, sliced
50 g ginger, julienned
500 ml coconut milk

375 ml coconut cream
200 g saluyot (wild spinach) leaves
2 tbsp patis (fish sauce)
1 tsp freshly ground black pepper

Blanch the bamboo shoots and squeeze to remove excess liquid, then place in a large pan. Add the crab, onion, ginger and coconut milk and bring to the boil.

Reduce heat and simmer for 20 minutes, then add the coconut cream and spinach and season with fish sauce and pepper.

Simmer for a further 3 minutes, then transfer to a platter and serve immediately.

SUGPO AT LAPU-LAPU SA HIBE AT KASUY
(sauté of prawns and grouper)

250 g fresh prawns
500 g lapu-lapu (grouper) fillets
sea salt and freshly ground pepper
125 ml cooking oil
2 tbsp olive oil
2 tbsp grated ginger
5 small onions, chopped
5 small tomatoes,
   skinned, seeded and chopped

50 g hibe (small dried shrimps),
   toasted and pounded to powder
200 g cashew nuts
   toasted and pounded to powder
250 ml coconut cream
2 chili peppers
2 tbsp freshly chopped coriander
fresh lime slices

Peel and de-vein the prawns, leaving the heads and tails attached. Season the fish and prawns with salt and pepper. Heat the oil in a pan until moderately hot and fry the fish for approximately 2 minutes on each side, then remove and transfer to a serving platter. Fry the prawns in the same oil for approximately 2 minutes, then place alongside the fish.

Meanwhile, heat the olive oil in a saucepan and sauté the ginger, onion and tomato for 2-3 minutes, then add the dried shrimp and ground cashew and continue to stir for a further 3 minutes.

Add the coconut cream, adjust seasoning to taste and stir until boiling point is reached, then remove pan from the heat and add the chili peppers and coriander. Pour hot sauce over the fish and prawns and garnish with slices of fresh lime

PUSIT PULUTAN (squid appetizer)

100 g dried squid, body parts only
250 ml cooking oil
1 large tomato
100 g green mango, julienned
100 g cucumber,
   seeded and julienned

50 g shallots, thinly sliced
1 tbsp chopped chili pepper
2 tbsp patis (fish sauce)
2 tbsp fresh calamansi juice
freshly ground pepper to taste

Broil sqid in pre-heated oven for 4 minutes, then, while still hot, pound with a mallet or pestle to separate fibers. Flake into matchstick pieces and fry in oil over medium heat until light brown and crispy. Drain on kitchen paper and set aside.

Cut tomato in half crosswise. Strain the seeds and juices to a bowl, squeezing to obtain at least 2 tbsp juice. Julienne remaining pulp and chill together with mango, cucumber, shallots and chili pepper.

In a bowl, just before serving, mix vegetables with fish sauce, calamansi juice, tomato juice and ground pepper, then remove excess liquid and toss in the fried squid.

TALAKITOK AT MAYA-MAYA SINIGANG SA MANGGA
(cavalla and red snapper in green mango broth)

500 g whole talakitok (cavalla)
500 g whole maya-maya
  (red snapper)
2 liters rice wash
300 g green mangoes,
  peeled and grated

200 g tomatoes,
  skinned and quartered
100 g spring onions,
  cut into 2 cm lengths
patis (fish sauce) to taste

Prepare the fish and cut each into 4-6 slices.

Pour the rice wash into a casserole, add the mango, tomato and spring onion and bring to the boil. Boil for 15 minutes, then add fish and allow to boil for a further 2 minutes.

Adjust seasonings and transfer to soup bowls. Serve immediately.

MANOK AT TREPANG (chicken stew with sea cucumber)

1 fresh chicken, quartered
1 tbsp soy sauce
200 g sea cucumber,
  boiled and sliced
125 g olive oil
2 tsp chopped ginger

100 g onions, chopped
0.5 tbsp sea salt
1 tsp freshly ground white pepper
2 tsp granulated sugar
375 ml chicken stock
2 tsp freshly chopped coriander

Marinate chicken in soy sauce for at least 1 hour, then drain. Heat the olive oil in a casserole brown chicken on all sides. Pour off excess oil, retaining about 3 tbsp and sauté the onion and ginger, then add the chicken, sea cucumber, salt and pepper

Continue to stir for a further 2 minutes, then add the sugar and stock and bring to the boil. Cover the casserole, reduce the heat and simmer until the chicken is tender. Finally, add the coriander and transfer to a serving platter.

Note: If using dried sea cucumber, soak overnight and scrape tough outer layer, then boil for at least 30 minutes.

MECHADO (braised beef à la mode)

1 kilo round steak
100 g pork backfat, in one strip
3 tbsp cooking oil
2 tbsp soy sauce
1 tbsp minced garlic
2 onions, diced

300 g tomatoes, quartered
125 g celery stalks, sliced
1 piece star anise
1 bay leaf
1.5 liter beef stock

With a larding needle, carefully insert pork fat into center of the beef. Shape the beef into a cylinder and truss with kitchen thread.

Heat the oil in a casserole and brown the beef on all sides, then add the garlic, soy sauce, onion, tomatoes, celery, star anise, bay leaf and beef stock. Cover and bring to the boil, then reduce the heat to a bare simmer and cook for approximately 4 hours, until the meat is tender, turning meat 3 or 4 times and adding more stock if necessary.

Remove meat and allow to cool and rest. Remove thread, cut meat into slices and transfer to a serving platter.

Strain the liquids from the casserole into a saucepan, removing as much fat as possible. Boil gently to reduce and thicken, then pour over the beef.

ENSALADANG LATO (seaweed salad)

1 kilo lato (seaweed)
200 g tomatoes, cut into wedges
150 g onions, sliced

75 ml olive oil
75 ml vinegar
0.5 tsp sea salt
0.5 tsp freshly ground black pepper

Wash the seaweed and discard the roots and wilted parts. Arrange in a salad bowl and garnish with the tomato and onion.

Mix together the oil, vinegar, salt and pepper and drizzle generously over the seaweed.

Note: If desired, top salad with crushed pork crackling, chopped cashew nuts or pan-toasted dried baby shrimps

MATAMIS NA PUGAD NG BALINSASAYAW
(sweet soup of bird's nest)

50 g bird's nest
250 g granulated sugar
zest of 1 dayap (lime)

175 g cantaloupe balls
175 g watermelon balls
180 g mango balls
150 ml coconut cream

Soak bird's nest overnight, then wash thoroughly under running water. Boil in 500 ml water for 30 minutes, then drain and set aside.
Place the sugar in a saucepan, add the lime zest and 1 liter water and bring to the boil. Cook for 15 minutes, then add the bird's nest and continue to boil for a further minute, until the syrup is thick.
Combine the fruits and bird's nest in a serving bowl, then add coconut cream.
Chill in the refrigerator for at least 30 minutes before serving.

Bicol Flavors

Mayon Volcano is the landmark of the Bicol region. It rises majestically, often shrouded by clouds at its peak, and revealing itself totally only on clear days. Mayon is still active, making its presence known periodically by rumblings and, once in a while, through a display of pyrotechnics.

Something else hot identified with the region is the sili, or hot chili pepper. Bicol is known for its spicy food and one such dish, Bicol Express, is named after the train that travels from Manila, because, it is said, a taste of this hot concoction makes you run for a glass of water.

However, there are other ingredients essential to Bicol cuisine, coconut milk and gabi (taro) being prominent among them. These two are brought together in *laing*, a dish flavored with shrimps.Coconut milk also features strongly, often combined with the pili nut, in the myriad of local sweets.

ALIMASAG AT LANGKA SA GATA
(crab with jackfruit in coconut cream)

500 ml coconut milk
300 g jackfruit meat, flaked
1 small onion, sliced
50 g ginger, julienned
6 pieces lemon grass,
    white part only, cut crosswise

2 tsp minced garlic
1 kilo crabs, quartered
sea salt and pepper to taste
500 ml coconut cream
100 g green chilies

Place the coconut milk, jackfruit, onion, ginger, lemon grass and garlic in a casserole and boil over a moderate heat for 10 minutes, then add the crabs and season to taste with salt and pepper. Reduce heat, cover and allow to simmer for a further 15-20 minutes. Set aside and keep hot.

Meanwhile, in a separate pan, bring the coconut cream to the boil and cook, stirring continuously, until the cream is thick enough to coat the ladle.

Pour the cream over the crab mixture, add the chilies and simmer for a further 5 minutes, then serve immediately.

KINUNOT NA PAGI (flaked stingray in hot spices)

*1 kilo stingray, yielding
   approximately 330 g of meat
1 onion
1 stalk celery
1 bay leaf
1 tsp black peppercorns
3 tbsp olive oil
125 g chopped onion*

*1 tbsp minced garlic
1 tbsp chopped ginger
1 tbsp chopped chili pepper
125 ml vinegar
125 ml coconut cream
sea salt to taste
freshly ground black pepper*

Clean the stingray thoroughly and blanch in boiling water for 1 minute. When cool, remove skin and cut into quarters.

Bring 1.5 liters of water to the boil, add the whole onion, celery, bay leaf and peppercorns and boil for 3 minutes, then add the quartered fish and allow to simmer for at least another 3 minutes. Remove fish, scrape off meat with a spoon and set aside.

Heat the oil in a pan and sauté the garlic for 2 minutes, then add the chopped onion, ginger, chili pepper and vinegar. Simmer for 10 minutes, then add the stingray meat and cook for a further 2 minutes.

Adjust seasonings to taste and add the coconut cream. Bring to the boil, then remove from heat and transfer to a serving dish.

POCHERO (boiled meat and vegetables)

1 kilo whole beef brisket
1 kilo whole chicken
500 g pork belly
175 g chorizo Bilbao
  (garlic sausage)
1.5 tbsp crushed garlic
200 g onions, quartered
1 tbsp whole peppercorns
2 bay leaves
400 g potatoes, peeled and quartered

400 g gabi (taro root),
  peeled and cut into slices
200 g saba (cooking bananas),
  halved diagonally
150 g green beans
400 g cabbage, cut into wedges
225 g chick peas, cooked or canned
sea salt and pepper to taste
1 tbsp olive oil

Place the beef, chicken, pork and sausage in a large casserole. Add the garlic, onion, peppercorns and bay leaves and cover with water. Bring to the boil and cook over a moderate heat. Remove the sausage after 30 minutes and remove other meats as they become tender. Keep warm.

Cook the vegetables in the broth, starting with the potatoes, then the taro, banana, green beans, cabbage and finally the chick peas.

Slice the meats and arrange with the vegetables in a serving dish, then drizzle with the olive oil and a little broth. Strain remaining broth and serve as a soup.

BICOL EXPRESS (pork ribs in spicy shrimp sauce)

1 kilo pork spareribs,
  cut into chunks
2 tbsp minced onion
2 tsp minced ginger
1 tsp minced garlic
2 stalks lemon grass,
  white part only, pounded
2 bay leaves
2 tbsp soy sauce

100 ml vinegar
750 ml coconut milk
freshly ground black pepper
10 hot chili peppers, finely diced
75 g bagoong alamang
  (shrimp paste)
250 ml coconut cream
100 g chili peppers

Place the pork ribs, onion, ginger, garlic, lemon grass, bay leaves, soy sauce, vinegar, coconut milk and pepper in a saucepan and bring to the boil. Cover and continue to boil for 5 minutes, then reduce the heat and allow to simmer for a further 40 minutes, or until the meat is tender.
Add the hot chili and shrimp paste and cook until the liquid is reduced by half. Add the coconut cream and chili peppers and continue to simmer until the oil separates from the cream, then transfer to a bowl and serve immediately..

LAING (taro leaves with shrimps in coconut cream)

300 g gabi (taro) leaves, shredded
200 g taro stalks, remove outer
  layer and cut into 5 cm lengths
250 g pork belly,
  boiled for 5 minutes and diced
200 g shrimps, shelled and deveined
1 onion, chopped
3 tbsp chopped ginger

125 g bagoong alamang
  (shrimp paste)
4 hot chilis, seeded and chopped
100 g chili peppers
1 tsp freshly ground black pepper
1 liter coconut milk
375 ml coconut cream

Arrange a layer of the gabi leaves and stalks in a deep pan.

Mix together pork, shrimps, onion, ginger, hot chili, shrimp paste and coconut milk and pour in to the pan. Cover with remaining leaves and stalks and season with freshly ground pepper.

Bring to the boil, then reduce heat and allow to simmer, without stirring, for 30 minutes. Add the chili peppers and coconut cream and simmer for a further 5 minutes, until the oil separates from the cream. Serve immediately.

Note: Do not stir at any time during cooking process.

ENSALADANG PUSO ng SAGING at KABUTE
(banana hearts and mushroom salad)

400 g puso ng saging
  (banana hearts)
2 tbsp sea salt
75 ml vinegar
2 tbsp diced red and green
  bell peppers
1 tbsp finely chopped onion

125 ml salad oil
0.5 tsp prepared mustard
0,5 tsp granulated sugar
sea salt to taste
freshly ground black pepper
100 g button mushrooms, quartered

Discard the outer parts of the banana hearts, leaving only the tender portion. Cut in half lengthwise.

Bring a pan of water to the boil, add the sea salt, all but 2 tsp vinegar and the banana hearts and boil for 12-15 minutes until tender. Allow to cool, then dice.

In a salad bowl, mix the peppers, onion, salad oil, mustard, sugar and remaining vinegar and season to taste with salt and pepper. Add the banana hearts and mushrooms and toss lightly.

MAZAPAN DE PILI (pili nut confection)

750 g pili nuts
  blanched, skinned and ground
200 g granulated sugar

250 g condensed milk
1 tsp vanilla
1 egg yolk, lightly beaten

Mix all the ingredients in a heavy pan and place over a moderate heat. Cook, stirring continuously, until the mixture holds together.

Allow to cool, then mold into desired shapes and brush with the egg yolk. Bake in a pre-heated, very slow oven (140° C) for 10 minutes, then set aside to cool before wrapping individually in candy papers.

MACAROONS (mini coconut buns)

450 g desiccated coconut
250 ml condensed milk
4 eggs, separated
75 g all-purpose flour

75 g clarified butter
1 tsp vanilla extract
2 tbsp raisins

In a bowl, mix together the coconut, condensed milk, egg yolks, flour, butter and vanilla extract and combine thoroughly.

In a separate bowl, beat the egg-whites until stiff peaks form, then fold into the coconut mixture.Put a teaspoon of the mixture into candy cases, top each with a raisin and arrange on a baking tray.

Bake in a pre-heated, moderately hot oven for 12-15 minutes, or until golden brown. Allow to cool before serving.

Central Visayas Flavors

Cebu may have all the amenities of a modern city but it hasn't lost its preference for simple flavors. The great variety of seafood - fish, shellfish or crustaceans are often prepared in three basic ways; marinated in vinegar, broiled or boiled.

The influence of Chinese cookery is strong in Cebu. *bam-i guisado*, stir-fry of two noodles, and *humba*, pork bellies braised in sugarcane, even have Chinese names while *escabechen tanguigue*, mackerel in garlic-turmeric sauce is a version of the Chinese sweet and sour.

The Spanish flavor is also very apparent, as with *tocino del cielo,* a rich caramel custard, and *tamalos,* a delicacy of rice with braised pork in a sesame-peanut sauce.

TANGUIGUE ESCABECHE (mackeral in garlic-turmeric sauce)

*4 tanguigue (mackeral) steaks,
  approximately 150 g each
2 tbsp fresh calamansi juice
sea salt and pepper
flour for dredging
75 ml cooking oil
small piece yellow ginger*

*3 cloves garlic, slivered
1 onion, sliced
50 g julienned bell pepper,
  red and green
2 tsp julienned ginger
125 ml vinegar
2 tbsp granulated sugar
250 ml fish stock*

Season the fish with calamansi juice, salt and pepper and dredge in flour. Pan-fry the fish in 75 ml oil and set aside.

Pound the yellow ginger, then add a few drops of water and squeeze to extract the juice.

In a fresh pan, heat the remaining oil and fry the garlic over a moderate heat until crispy, then remove and drain on absorbent kitchen paper.

Add the onion, bell peppers and the julienned ginger to the same pan and sauté for 3 minutes, then add the ginger juice, vinegar, sugar and stock and bring to the boil.

Reduce heat and simmer for 5 minutes, then adjust seasoning to taste, add the fish steaks and garlic and continue to cook for a further minute.

TAMALOS (peanut sesame tamales with pork)

1 kilo liempo (pork belly), skin on
2 tbsp minced garlic
500 ml vinegar
3 tbsp soy sauce
2 bay leaves
2 tbsp sea salt
1 tsp whole peppercorns

200 g peanuts, toasted
100 g sesame seeds, toasted
4 chili peppers
4 tbsp annato oil
200 g rice flour
8 banana leaves,
   approximately 25 cm square

Place the pork in a casserole, together with half the garlic, the vinegar, soy sauce, bay leaves, salt, peppercorns and 1.5 liters water. Bring to the boil and cook for 20 minutes, then remove pork from the broth and allow to rest. Slice pork into eight equal portions, return to the broth and simmer until tender. Remove and drain. Reserve the broth.

In a food processor, grind peanuts, sesame seeds, chili peppers, add the broth in a slow stream to produce a smooth paste.

In a saucepan, heat the annato oil and sauté the garlic briefly, then add peanut-sesame paste and cook, stirring continuously, until thick. Add the rice flour dispersed in 500 ml water and stir well, then immediately remove from heat.

For each tamalo, place 2 layers of the banana leaves on a flat surface. Pour 170 ml of the mixture in the center, add 2 pieces of pork and top with 100 ml more of the mixture. Hold the two sides of the banana leaves and fold together to secure, then clasp both ends to form a compact parcel. Using kitchen thread, tie a knot at one end and proceed to tie a loop crosswise around the mid-section, then make another knot at the opposite end to secure the parcel. Cook in a steamer for 45 minutes.

HUMBA (braised pork belly)

1 kilo liempo (pork belly), skin on　　*2 bay leaves*
175 ml vinegar　　*1 tbsp tajure (salted bean curd),*
60 ml soy sauce　　　*mashed*
1 tbsp salted black beans　　*1 tsp freshly ground black pepper*
75 g raw peanuts, shelled　　*35 g brown sugar*
1 tbsp minced garlic

Parboil whole bork belly in 750 ml water for 10 minutes, then cut into 6 equal portions. Reserve the broth.

With a sharp knife, carefully score skin side of each portion making criss-cross slits, approximately 1 cm apart and 0.5 cm deep, then place in a bowl with all the remaining ingredients and marinate in the refrigerator overnight.
Bring the reserved broth to the boil, add the pork with the remaining ingredients and cook for 1½ hours, until the meat is fork tender.

ADOBONG MANOK (chicken stew)

1.2 kilo fresh chicken　　*2 bay leaves*
125 ml vinegar　　*1 tsp crushed peppercorns*
50 ml soy sauce　　*1 tsp sea salt*
1 tbsp minced garlic　　*oil for frying*

Cut the chicken into serving-size pieces and place in a casserole. Add remaining ingredients, apart from the oil, together with 250 ml water and bring to the boil. Reduce heat and simmer for 40-50 minutes, then remove chicken and strain the stock.

In a frying pan, brown the chicken pieces in hot oil until crispy on all sides, then drain on absorbent paper and transfer to a platter. Reheat the stock and reduce to a thick, flowing consistency, then pour over chicken and serve immediately.

To make crisp abodo flakes, de-bone the chicken and flake the meat. Drizzle with sauce, transfer to a baking tray and spread evenly, then let stand for at least 1 hour. Fry in a wok with very little oil over a low heat, stirring continuously, for 30-45 minutes, until chicken meat is dry, brown and crisp.

BAMI-I-GUISADO - HUMBA

BAM-I GUISADO (sauté of two noodles)

100 g fresh shrimps
1 tbsp cooking oil
1.5 litres chicken stock
3 tbsp annato oil
0.5 tbsp minced garlic
1 onion, sliced
100 g boiled pork, sliced
2 chorizo Macao, sliced diagonally
  (Chinese pork sausage)
5 g wood ear mushroom,
  soaked and cut into strips

50 g carrots, sliced
200 g sotanghon noodles
  (mng bean noodles)
100 g cabbage, sliced
500 g fresh egg noodles
sea salt to taste
freshly ground black pepper
2 hard boiled eggs, sliced
1 tpsp finely chopped spring onion
1 tbsp crispy fried garlic

Shell and de-vein the shrimps and fry the heads in a saucepan. Add stock and boil for 5 minutes, then process in a blender and strain.

Heat the annato oil in a large pan and sauté the garlic and onion, then add, one at a time, the shrimps, pork, sausage, mushroom, carrot, mung bean noodles and cabbage. Mix well, then add reserved broth and bring to boil.

Cook for 5 minutes, then add the egg noodles, toss and continue to cook for a further 3 minutes. Adjust seasonings to taste, then transfer to a serving platter and garnish with slices of hard boiled egg, chopped spring onion and crispy-fried garlic.

ENSALADANG MAIS (corn salad)

250 g grated coconut
50 g ginger, minced
100 ml vinegar
500 g corn kernels, scraped from
  fresh boiled corn on the cob
300 g tomatoes, diced

300 g eggplant, broiled, peeled and
  cut, crosswise, into 2 cm slices
150 g onions, diced
1 tbsp sea salt
1 tsp freshly ground pepper
100 g chicharon (pork crackling),
  crushed

In a bowl, mash grated coconut, ginger and vinegar and squeeze over a strainer to extract juices. Set aside in the refrigerator for at least 30 minutes.

Combine remaining ingredients, apart from the crackling, in a salad bowl. Add the coconut extract and toss lightly, then garnish with crushed crackling.

MANGGA AT SAGO (mango and tapioca pearls)

3 ripe mangoes
100 g tapioca pearls
125 g brown sugar
175 ml coconut cream

75 g granulated sugar
0.25 tsp ground cinnamon
4 pandan leaves

Cut the mangoes in half and scoop the flesh into small balls. Reserve the skins.

Boil the tapioca in 1.25 liters water, stirring continuously for 20 minutes, then drain and wash under cold running water. Place in a bowl and set aside.

Place brown sugar in a saucepan, add 250 ml water and the pandan leaves and boil for 10 minutes, stirring continuously, then strain and allow to cool. Add the tapioca and place in refrigerator to chill.

Pour coconut cream into a fresh saucepan, add granulated sugar and cinnamon and boil until the sugar has completely dissolved. Add pandan leaves and allow sauce to thicken, then remove from heat and discard pandan leaves. Set aside to cool, then chill in the refrigerator.

To serve, mix the mango balls and tapioca and spoon into the reserved skins, then drizzle with the sweetened coconut cream.

TOCINO DEL CIELO (egg yolk caramel custard)

1.2 kilos granulated sugar
570 g egg yolks,
  approximately 30 yolks

75 ml clarified butter
1 tsp vanilla extract

Place 200 g sugar in a heavy saucepan and heat gently until dissolved. Increase heat and boil without stirring, until caramel in color. Immediately pour into a 23 cm pan, swirling the caramel around to cover the entire bottom. Set aside.

In a fresh saucepan, combine the remaining sugar with 750 ml water and cook over a moderate heat until it bubbles. The syrup should not take on any color.

Place the egg yolks in a large mixing bowl and whisk until frothy, then slowly add the syrup and continue to whisk. When the syrup is completely incorporated add clarified butter and vanilla extract, then strain mixture into the pan and steam for 45 minutes.

Western Visayas Flavors

Ilongo means both the people and the language of Negros Occidental and Iloilo. Sugar is synonymous with the fortunes of the people so sweets are an important part of the cuisine. They range from simple delights, such as *baye-baye,* a sweet dough made from sticky rice, to very refined pastries. *Guinataan halo-halo*, a mix of fruits and yam in coconut cream, is popular everywhere.

Lumpia Ubod, crepes of heart of palm, which originate from Silay, are so popular that large quantities are air-shipped to Manila almost daily. Another famous local dish is *pancit molo*, which originated in the town of Molo in the province of Iloilo.

Like all Visayans, Ilongos favor raw seafood marinated only in vinegar, such as the popular mackerel dish, *kilawin tanguigue. Inasal na manok*, a barbecued chicken, marinated in a garlic-annato mixture is another dish likely to be served throughout the region.

LUMBIA UBOD (crepes of heart of palm)

1 kilo ubod (heart of palm)
2 tbsp milk
3 tbsp cooking oil
1tbsp minced garlic
1 large onion, sliced
200 g pork, boiled and julienned
125 g shrimps, shelled, de-veined
  and halved lengthwise
1 tbsp granulated sugar
sea salt and pepper to taste
20 lettuce leaves
minced garlic
ground peanuts

Wrappers:
3 eggs
225 g all-purpose flour
75 ml oil
dash of salt

Sauce:
50 g cornstarch
125 soy sauce
250 g brown sugar

Julienne the heart of palm and, to prevent discoloration, soak in a mixture of the milk and 300 ml water, then drain thoroughly.

Heat the oil in a saucepan and sauté the garlic and onion, then add the pork, shrimps. heart of palm and sugar and season with salt and pepper.Cook over a moderate heat for 20 minutes, then strain to remove excess liquid and set aside to cool.

To serve, lay a wrapper on a flat surface and place a lettuce leaf on top, then add a portion of the heart of palm mixture along the centre of the leaf. Roll up once, fold in at one end and continue to roll up, leaving the leaf protruding from the other end. Serve with side dishes of minced garlic, ground peanuts and lumpia sauce.

To make the wrappers, sift the flour and salt into a bowl, add the eggs, oil and 625 ml water and blend well until the batter is smooth. Place a 15 cm, non-stick pan over a moderate heat and add 2 Tbsp batter. Tilt the pan to cover the flat surface completely and cook until set. Cook the remaining wrappers and stack to cool.

To make the sauce, first dissolve cornstarch in a mixture of sugar, soy sauce and 625 ml water and bring to boil until the mixture thickens and the cornstrach. is thoroughly cooked.

PANCIT MOLO (stuffed noodle soup)

1 kilo chicken necks and backs
1 chicken breast
2 onions, chopped
2 sticks celery, chopped
1 tbsp black peppercorns
125 g ground pork
125 g shrimps,
*   shelled, de-veined and chopped*

2 tbsp chopped kinchay
*   (Chinese parsley)*
0.5 tsp sea salt
0.25 tsp freshly ground pepper
30 molo (wonton) wrappers
3 tbsp cooking oil
50 g minced garlic
100 g ham, cut into fine strips
2 tbsp finely chopped spring onion

Place the chicken parts, half the onion, the celery and peppercorns and cover with 3 litres water and bring to the boil. Reduce heat, cover the pan and allow to simmer for 1 hour, then remove the chicken breast and flake the meat. Strain the broth.

In a bowl, combine the pork, shrimp and kinchay and season to taste with salt and pepper. Mix thoroughly.

Lay a molo wrapper on a flat surface and place one-half teaspoon of mixture in one corner. Fold the corner over the mixture and roll halfway towards the center. Lift wrapper holding the rolled portion between the edges of the filling with the fingers of both hands. Fold both sides inward, one side overlapping the other, to form a cone with two pointed sides. Paste the folded sides together with a dab of egg-yolk. Repeat process with remaining wrappers.

Heat the oil in a pan and fry the garlic until golden and crispy, then remove, drain on absorbent paper and set aside. Add remaining onion to the pan, together with the flaked chicken, ham and reserved broth and bring to the boil.

Drop in the molo 'pouches' and cook for 3 minutes, then transfer to individual soup plates and top each with the crispy-fried garlic and chopped spring onion.

KINILAW na TANGUIGUE (mackerel in coconut vinaigrette)

500 g tanguigue (mackerel) fillets
250 ml vinegar
250 g grated coconut
6 shallots, sliced
2 tbsp chopped ginger

2 chili peppers, seeded and chopped
2 tsp sea salt
0.5 tsp freshly ground black pepper
Onion rings for garnish

Cut the fish into 2 cm cubes and wash in half the vinegar. In a non-reactive bowl, combine remaining vinegar and grated coconut, then extract the juice and strain into a glass bowl. Add the fish cubes, shallot, ginger, chili, salt and pepper.

Chill in the refrigerator, then transfer to a platter and garnish with onion rings.

INASAL NA MANOK (garlic-annato roast chicken)

1 kilo fresh chicken, quartered   *2 tbsp fresh calamansi juice*
2 tbsp minced garlic   *1 tsp freshly ground black pepper*
1 tbsp sea salt   *3 tbsp annato oil*

Mix together the garlic, salt, pepper, calamansi juice and annato oil and rub over the chicken, then place in the refrigerator overnight. Reserve marinade.

When ready to cook, skewer the chicken on bamboo sticks and cook slowly over a charcoal fire for approximately 1 hour, turning the chicken once and basting occasionally with the reserved marinade

INASAL NA MANOK - KINILAW NA TANGUIGUE

PATA AT KADIOS (pork knuckle with pigeon peas)

1 pata (front pork knuckle), sliced
3 tbsp cooking oil
100 g onions, chopped
1 tbsp minced garlic
200 g tomatoes, chopped
225 g kadios
 (black or green pigeon peas)
  soaked overnight and drained

600 g green langka (jackfruit),
  cut into strips
100 g malunggay
  (horseradish) leaves,
sea salt to taste
freshly ground black pepper

Soak the beans overnight, then drain thoroughly.

Heat the oil in a casserole and sauté the garlic, onion and tomatoes, then add the knuckles, beans and 2.5 liters of water. Bring to the boil, then reduce heat and allow to simmer until the meat and beans are tender.

Add the jackfruit and continue to simmer for a further 5 minutes, then add the horseradish leaves and season to taste with salt and freshly ground pepper.

GUINATAAN HALO-HALO (fruit and yam stew)

250 g glutinous rice flour
1.5 liters coconut milk
6 pandan leaves
225 g camote (sweet potato), cubed
225 g gabi (taro root), cubed
225 g ube (purple yam), cubed

6 saba (cooking bananas), sliced
250 g ripe langka (jackfruit),
  cut into strips crosswise
200 g cooked sago pearls
300 g granulated sugar
250 ml coconut cream

Combine the rice flour with 250 ml water and form into small balls.

Place the coconut milk and pandan leaves in a casserole and bring to the boil, then add the sago, sweet potato, taro and yam. Cook for 5 minutes, then add the banana, jackfruit and rice balls and continue to cook over a moderate heat until all the rice balls float to the surface.

Discard the pandan leaves and stir in sugar and coconut cream, then transfer to a serving bowl.

Davao Flavors

The best place to savor Davao flavors is in one of its many markets, bursting at the seams with seafoods, meats, fruits and vegetables. The produce of Davao is bountiful and the cooking methods are simple enough to bring out their quality. Broiled tuna jaws, Davao's claim to culinary fame, is unmatched elsewhere.

Because the region is a top producer of quality meats and poultry, the dishes are stout and hearty. And few places produce the range of fruits from the mundane banana to that most exotic of fruits, the durian. Those who have not developed a taste for the raw flesh of that most controversial fruit durian should sample the *pastel de durian*, delicate durian tarts.

SINIGANG NA SUGPO (prawns in sour broth)

500 g fresh prawns
100 g green tamarind
175 g tomatoes, quartered
100 g onions, diced
1.5 liters rice wash
200 g puso ng saging (banana
  hearts), tender parts only, sliced

100 g radish, sliced diagonally
100 g string beans,
  cut into 5 cm lengths
125 g eggplant, sliced diagonally
75 g kangkong (water cabbage)
100 g chili peppers
patis (fish sauce) to taste

Shell and de-vein prawns but leave heads and tails attached.

Boil the tamarind in 250 ml water until tender, then mash and pass through a strainer. Reserve the liquid and discard the solids.

In a large pot, boil the tomato, onion, rice wash and tamarind water. Reduce the heat, add the banana heart, radish, string beans and eggplant and simmer for 8-10 minutes.

Add the prawns, water cabbage and chili peppers and continue to simmer for a further 2 minutes, then season to taste with fish sauce. Transfer to a soup tureen and serve immediately.

ADOBONG PUSIT (squid with vinegar, garlic and peppercorns)

1 kilo small squids
3 tbsp olive oil
2 tbsp minced garlic
125 ml vinegar

75 ml soy sauce
1 tsp freshly ground black pepper
2 bay leaves
2 chili peppers

Clean the squids thoroughly under running water, then detach the heads from the body, keeping the ink sacs intact. Discard the stiff membranes.

Heat the oil in a casserole and fry the garlic until brown then add the squid and stir-fry for 1 minute. Break the ink sacs into the casserole and add the vinegar, soy sauce, pepper and bay leaves.

Reduce heat and simmer for 10 minutes, then add the chili peppers and transfer to a serving dish.

UKOY (shrimp and sweet potato fritters)

200 g small shrimps
300 g camote (sweet potaoes),
    julienned
3 egg-whites

75 g cornstarch
salt and pepper to taste
oil for frying

Wash shrimps, remove the heads and place in a bowl, then add the sweet potato, and egg-whites. Mix the cornstarch with a small quantity of cold water and add to the bowl, then season to taste with salt and pepper and stir to blend. Drain and remove excess liquid.

Heat the oil in a shallow frying pan and drop in a tablespoonful of the mixture and press with a spatula to flatten. Repeat process to fry a few fritters at a time. Fry until golden brown and crispy, then drain off excess oil on absorbent paper. Serve with a garlic-vinegar dip.

MORCON (stuffed beef roulade)

500 g whole round steak,
sea salt and freshly ground pepper
50 g carrots, cut into batonnete
50 g celery, cut into batonnete
1 chorizo Bilbao (garlic sausage),
* cut into batonnete*
1 whole pickle, cut into batonnete
50 g sliced bacon

2 tbsp all-purpose flour
75 ml cooking oil
1 onion, chopped
1 tbsp minced garlic
200 g tomatoes, sliced
250 ml tomato sauce
2 bay leaves
1 liter beef stock

Slice the beef into a thin sheet and season with salt and pepper. On one end of the beef, arrange the carrot, celery, sausage, pickle and bacon, Then, roll the meat to form a cylinder and truss with kitchen thread. Dredge in flour. Heat the oil and brown the meat on all sides.

Add the onion, garlic, tomato, tomato sauce and bay leaf to the casserole and stir over a fairly high heat until the liquids have reduced, then add the stock and bring back to the boil.

Add the beef, reduce heat to a bare simmer and cook for 4 hours, until tender. Remove the beef and cut into slices, approximately 15 mm thick, and arrange on a serving plate. Strain sauce, re-heat and pour over the meat.

ENSALADANG SUHA (pomelo radish salad)

2 tbsp vinegar
100 ml olive oil
1 tsp prepared mustard
0.5 tsp granulated sugar

sea salt to taste
freshly ground black pepper
1 whole pomelo
300 g radish, julienned

Place the vinegar, olive oil, mustard, sugar, salt and pepper in a bowl and blend with a wire whisk.

Peel the pomelo and flake the wedges, then combine in a salad bowl with the radish and toss lightly with the dressing.

GULAMAN AT BUKO SA PANDAN (coconut jelly dessert)

3 tbsp unflavored gelatin
625 ml buko (young coconut) water
200 g granulated sugar
100 g pandan leaves
  (or 1 tsp pandan essence)

green and yellow food colorings
200 ml all-purpose cream, chilled
200 g buko (young coconut) milk
3 tbsp condensed milk
125 ml coconut cream

Add gelatin to half the coconut water and stir, then set aside.In a saucepan, boil the remaining coconut water with the pandan leaves and sugar. Reduce heat and simmer for 5 minutes, then add gelatin mixture and bring back to the boil until gelatin is completely dissolved. Add 2 drops green and 1 drop yellow food coloring. Pour mixture into a 2 liter pan, allow to cool, then cut into 15 mm cubes.

Pour the cream into a bowl and beat until thick, then add the condensed milk and coconut and stir to blend. Refrigerate for 20 minutes.

Spoon the gelatin cubes into tall glasses and add a layer of the coconut mixture. Continue to add layers until the glass is full, ending with a topping of coconut. mixture. Add a little coconut cream before serving.

PASTELITOS DE MANGOSTEEN (mangosteen tarts)

375 ml fresh milk
375 ml all-purpose cream
350 g mangosteen jam
6 egg yolks, lightly beaten
175 g granulated sugar
75 g flour
75 ml light syrup
150 g cashew nuts, chopped

Pastry shells:
375 g all-purpose flour
150 g granulated sugar
pinch of sea salt
300 g butter
3 eggs yolks, beaten

Pour the milk and cream into a saucepan and cook over a medium heat, then add the jam, egg yolks, sugar, flour and syrup and mix well. Bring to the boil, then lower heat and simmer until the mixture thickens. Set aside to cool.

To make the pastry, mix flour, sugar and salt in a bowl, then cut in the butter and work with the fingers, until the mixture resembles coarse crumbs. Add the eggs and toss lightly until dough holds together. . With hands, shape dough into a ball, wrap in plastic film and chill in refrigerator for at least 30 minutes, then divide into 40 pieces and press into tartlet molds.

Spoon a little filling into each shell and top with chopped cashews, then bake in moderately-hot oven (200° C) for 10 minutes, until the pastry is golden brown.

PASTEL DE DURIAN (durian tarts)

375 ml fresh milk
375 ml all-purpose cream
125 g granulated sugar
5 egg yolks
3 tbsp light syrup
3 tbsp flour
100 g mashed durian flesh

Shells:
375 g all-purpose flour
150 g granulated sugar
pinch of sea salt
300 g butter
1 egg, beaten

Place a pan over medium heat, add the milk, cream, sugar, egg yolks, syrup and flour and whisk until smooth. Bring to boiling point and cook until a thick consistency is reached. Set aside to cool, then add durian and stir to blend.

To make the pastry, combine the flour, sugar and salt in a bowl and cut in the butter. Work with the fingers until the mixture resembles coarse crumbs. Add eggs and toss lightly until the dough holds together, then wrap in plastic film and refrigerate for at least 30 minutes.

Divide three-quarters of the dough into 30 pieces and press into tartlet molds and bake in a moderately-hot oven (200° C) until lightly browned, then fill with the durian. Cut remaining dough into strips and arrange in a lattice design on the top of the durian, then bake for a further 25 minutes.

101

Zamboanga Flavors

The language of Zamboanga is a local patois with heavy Spanish roots called Chabacano, The cuisine of Zamboanga is the same. The strong influence of Spanish colonial cooking is evident in such dishes as *callos*, ox tripe and knuckles in garlic-tomato sauce, *maja blanca*, a blancmange of corn and coconut cream. On the other hand, the influence of Malay cooking is clearly demonstrated with the recipe for *guinataang curacha*, local crabs roasted in a rich coconut sauce.

The crabs called curacha are indigenous to Zamboanga and are prized for the sweetness of the meat. Long ago someone wailed, "Don't you go, don't you go to far Zamboanga". He must have wanted to keep for himself all the curacha and other myriad delights of that wonderful place.

GUINATAANG CURACHA (crabs in roasted coconut sauce)

6 curacha (Zamboanga crabs),
* halved*
2 coconuts, grated
100 g yellow ginger, grated

3 tbsp patis (fish sauce)
1 tsp freshly ground black pepper
3 tbsp chopped chili pepper
6 whole chili peppers

Spread grated coconut evenly on a metal tray and broil in a moderately hot oven (200° C), as close as possible to broiler, for 3 minutes or until top is golden brown. Allow to cool and wrap in cheese cloth, then squeeze to extract at least 250 ml coconut cream. Set aside. Add 750 ml water to the remaining pulp and squeeze further to extract lighter coconut milk.

Pour the coconut milk in a casserole, add the onion, ginger, and chopped chili peppers and bring to the boil, then reduce the heat and allow to simmer for 3 minutes. Add the crabs and season and season with fish sauce and pepper.

Simmer for a further 15 minutes, then stir in coconut cream and whole chili peppers. Remove from heat and transfer to a serving dish.

MALASUGUE sa BAGON GATA (swordfish with coconut sauce)

6 malasugue (swordfish) fillets
approximately 175 g each
2 tbsp fresh calamansi juice
1 tbsp sea salt
1 tsp freshly ground black pepper
2 tsp freshly sliced spring onion

Bagon Gata sauce:
250 g bagoong alamang
(shrimp paste)
75 ml olive oil
150 g onions, chopped
50 g ginger, chopped
150 g tomatoes, chopped
50 g chili peppers, chopped
500 ml coconut cream

Wash the fish and season with calamansi juice, salt and pepper. Cook under a hot grill, then transfer to a serving platter, coat with the prepared sauce and and top with the freshly sliced spring onion.

To make the sauce, add hot water to the shrimp paste , then strain to remove excess saltiness. Heat the oil in a pan and saute the onion, ginger and tomato, then add shrimp paste and chili and continue to cook over a moderate heat for a further 3 minutes. Finally, add coconut cream, let boil and remove from heat.

ESTOFADONG MANOK (chicken stew in red wine)

1 kilo chicken thighs
250 ml red wine
1 bay leaf
1 tbsp sea salt
1 tsp freshly ground black pepper
75 ml olive oil
100 g slab bacon, cut into chunks
1 tbsp minced garlic
100 g shallots

250 g tomatoes, chopped
100 g garlic sausage,
sliced diagonally
100 g button mushrooms
50 g black olives
500 ml chicken stock
3 fried bananas,
cut in half diagonally

Marinate the chicken in wine, bay leaf, salt and pepper for 6 hours, then drain and reserve marinade.

In a skillet, brown chicken in olive oil on all sides, then remove. Add the bacon and allow fat to render, then remove. Add garlic, shallots and tomato and saute for 2 minutes, then add sausage, mushrooms, olives and replace chicken and bacon. Simmer for 5 minutes, then add stock and marinade and bring to a boil.

Cook for a further 30 minutes, until chicken is tender, then transfer to a serving dish and garnish with fried bananas.

CALLOS (ox tripe and knuckles in garlic tomato sauce)

1 kilo ox tripe
1 kilo ox knuckles
250 g slab of bacon
2 pieces chorizo Bilbao
  (garlic sausage)
1 small onion, quartered
2 sticks celery, with leaves
6 cloves garlic
1 tbsp black peppercorns
sprig of parsley

2 tbsp olive oil
2 tbsp chopped onion
1 tbsp minced garlic
200 g tomatoes,
  skinned, seeded and chopped
200 g can pimentos, cut into strips
400 g chick peas,
  boiled and skinned
2 tbsp paprika
1 tsp freshly ground black pepper
50 g grated parmesan cheese

Place the tripe, knuckles, bacon, sausage, quartered onions, celery, whole garlic cloves, peppercorns and parsley in a large pot and add sufficient water to cover.

Bring to the boil, then reduce to a simmer and skim off the froth as it comes to the surface. Remove the sausage after 30 minutes and the other meats, including tripe, as they become tender. De-bone the knuckle and cut into chunks. Cut tripe and bacon in a similar way. Cut sausage in half lengthwise, then diagonally. Strain the stock and set aside.

Pour the oil in a large casserole and fry bacon to allow fat to render, then remove bacon and drain on kitchen paper. Add the minced garlic, chopped onion and tomato to the pan and sauté until the liquid is significantly reduced, then re-place bacon, add the other meats, pimento, chick peas, paprika, pepper and 1 liter reserved stock and bring to the boil.

Reduce heat and allow to simmer for 15-20 minutes, then stir in the cheese and adjust seasonings to taste. Serve immediately.

ENSALADANG AGAR-AGAR AT MANGGANG HILAW
(seaweed and green mango salad)

250 g agar-agar (fresh seaweed)
200 g green mangoes, sliced
4 tomatoes, seeded and chopped
100 g shallots, sliced

125 ml vinegar
1 tbsp patis (fish sauce)
1 tsp granulated sugar

Arrange the seaweed, mango, tomato and shallot in a salad bowl.

Combine the vinegar, fish sauce and sugar and drizzle generously over the salad.

ENSALADANG LANZONES (lanzones salad)

300 g lanzones (see margin)
200 g pomelo
200 g ubod (heart of plam),
  julienned
50 g leek, julienned

Dressing:
125 ml extra virgin olive oil
4 tbsp dayab (lime) juice
2 tbsp patis
0,5 tsp honey
freshly ground black pepper

Peel the lanzones and separate into sections, discarding the sections with large stones. Peel pomelo wedges and break into chunks. Arrange the fruits in a salad bowl, together with the heart of palm and leek.

Combine the olive oil, lime juice, fish sauce, pepper and honey and drizzle generously over the salad.

MAJA BLANCA (blancmange of corn and coconut cream)

750 g corn kernels,
  scraped from the cob
1 liter coconut milk
350 g granulated sugar
2 tbsp butter

1 tsp pandan essence
250 g cornstarch
1 egg yolk
1 tbsp toasted coconut flakes

In a blender, process the corn, coconut milk, sugar, butter, pandan essence and cornstarch until smooth, then transfer to a saucepan and cook over a moderate heat for 30 minutes, stirring continuously.

Whisk in the egg yolk, remove pan from heat and pour mixture into a pudding mold. Chill in the refrigerator, then transfer to a serving platter and garnish with toasted coconut flakes.

FLAN CON MERENGUE (custard with meringue)

250 g white granulated sugar
10 egg yolks
400 g evaporated milk
250 g granulated sugar
zest of 1 lemon

Meringue:
2 egg-whires
75 g granulated sugar

In a pan, caramelize the sugar over a low heat , then pour the syrup into an oven-proof baking dish and swirl to spread evenly.

Beat the egg yolks and gradually add the evaporated milk and sugar, then stir in lemon zest. Strain the mixture into the caramel-lined dish, place in a bain marie and bake in a pre-heated, moderate oven for 30-40 minutes.

Meanwhile, make the meringue. Beat the egg whites, gradually the sugar until stiff peaks are formed.
Remove flan from oven and spread meringue on top, then return to oven and bake for a further 10 minutes, until the peaks in meringue turn golden brown. Chill before serving.